THE
CLADDAGH
RING

THE
CLADDAGH
RING

IRELAND'S CHERISHED SYMBOL
of FRIENDSHIP, LOYALTY AND LOVE

Malachy McCourt

RUNNING PRESS
PHILADELPHIA · LONDON

TABLE OF CONTENTS

INTRODUCTION

T HERE IS IN Ireland a place called Claddagh, simply
pronounced *Klada*, which nestles in close proxim-
ity to the sea and to the university city of Galway.
A hardy breed of fisherfolk inhabit this little hamlet, having
managed to maintain their odd individuality for many centuries. And when they've had to emigrate, they have always
sought their own kin so that excessive use of language is not
called for in everyday communication. How is it, then, that a
ring—the Claddagh ring—is named after and will always be
associated with this once remote and isolated fishing village?
A ring so simple in its visual statement that the mere presentation of it to one's beloved takes away all need for words.
The plain gold wedding cingulum indicates an eternity of
attachment regardless of exigencies, whereas the Claddagh
ring symbolically pledges not only everlasting love, but fealty,
loyalty, trust, faith. Its motto, "Let love and friendship reign,"
is there to see in the sight of a heart being caressed by loving
hands, and capstoned by a simple crown. There are many legends about the origins of the Claddagh ring's design and its

Galway associations. It is said that the combination of hands, heart, and crown is the coat of arms of the Joyce family, and the famous James who may not have set foot in Galway did marry a native of the Claddagh region, one Nora Barnicle, thus getting close to his roots. Neither of these lovers were known to possess a ring, but other famous and infamous fools, clowns, hypocrites, and pseudo-Irish have been known to sport this pure symbol of love and friendship. Queen (we are not amused) Victoria proudly exhibited her ring made in Ireland even as millions of the misfortunate were dying of a man-induced starvation program. Her son Edward VII, it was said, was fond of this ring too. Other people in their millions can't wait to get a finger in their very own rings, particularly as it was bruited about that a bricklayer's daughter, Grace Kelly, who married a gambling casino operator, self-styled Prince Ranier, were showing off their rings to anyone who would look and listen. Wearing the ring didn't do much for Ronald Reagan, the forgetful president, and history will record the love lives of John F. Kennedy and Bill Clinton, who claim Irish heritage and love for the ring and its aura.

There seem to be no demarcation lines between the types of people who buy and wear and give this ring. It's fashionable among liars, loonies, rockers like U2, wild men like Oasis, actresses like Julia Roberts, Jennifer Aniston, and Mia Farrow, and now—get this—the rapper community have seized and are pledging their troth with an exchange of Claddagh rings.

As well as evoking noble sentiments from mature and spiritually exalted human beings, falling in love can also evoke drivel and doggerel from slobbery would-be poets and dreary sentimentality, enough to make a person vomit, and so the Irish do endure the likes of Galway Bay and the Old Claddagh Ring because the spirit of the ring makes it easy to forgive these atrocious insults to the Muse.

How the ring came to be a part of our history and lore, our life and love, is something of a mystery well worth exploring, and that's what this tome is about. It's a loving look at a loving and universal symbol of the best of the heart, the head, the hands, and the invisible soul of humanity. May your heart be clasped by the hands of your beloved, and may your days be crowned with happiness, and occasional bouts of ecstasy.

—Malachy McCourt
New York City
April 2003

ACKNOWLEDGMENTS

T HANKS ARE DUE to Jonathan Margetts of T. Dillon & Sons—Galway's Original Makers of the Claddagh Ring (est. 1750), and his staff at The Claddagh Museum, for their assistance in the research for this book. I'd also like to thank Tom Kenny of Kenny's Bookshop and Art Galleries Ltd. in Galway, and Dorothy King for their generous assistance. Several books were enormously valuable as sources for this book, most notably *Down by the Claddagh* by Peader O'Dowd, *Rain on the Wind* by Walter Macken, *The Claddagh Ring Story* by Cecily Joyce, *A History of Ireland* by Mike Cronin, and *The Story of the Claddagh Ring* by Sean McMahon.

The Old Claddagh Ring

by Patrick B. Kelly

The Old Claddagh ring, sure it was my grandmother's,
She wore it a lifetime and gave it to me;
All through the long years, she wore it so proudly,
It was made where the Claddagh rolls down to the sea.
What tales it could tell of trials and hardships,
And of grand happy days when the whole world could sing—
So away with your sorrow, it will bring love tomorrow,
Everyone loves it, the Old Claddagh Ring.

With the crown and the crest to remind me of honour,
And clasping the heart that God's blessing would bring,
The circle of gold always kept us contented,
'Twas true love entwined in the Old Claddagh Ring.
As she knelt at her prayers and thought of her dear ones,
Her soft, gentle smile would charm a king;
And on her worn hand as she told me the story,
You could see the bright glint of the Old Claddagh Ring.

It was her gift to me and it made me so happy,
With this on my finger my heart it would sing;
No king on his throne could be half so happy
As I am when I'm wearing my Old Claddagh Ring.
When the angels above call me up to heaven
In the heart of the Claddagh their voices will sing
Saying "Away with your sorrow, you'll be with us tomorrow,
Be sure and bring with you the Old Claddagh Ring."

CHAPTER I

When the angels above call me up to heaven

The Claddagh Heart Breaks

I T WAS JUST a day after the terrorist attacks on the World Trade Center in New York on September 11, with fires still burning beneath the rubble. All over Manhattan, scores of anxious people were taping pictures of their friends and loved ones on walls, subway stations, on the sides of phone booths, any available flat surface. Hundreds of photographs formed heartbreaking collages at many of these shrines, where fellow citizens came to stare solemnly at the photographs of disappeared human beings of all ethnic groups and nationalities, and then drifted quietly away. The city and its people still had hope, and this hope was reflected in the diligence and desperation of those pasting the signs. In their minds, and ours too, there had to be survivors, and the only thing they could do was put the word out that their friend or loved one had not returned home from work.

The faces, so full of life in these pictures, appeared with descriptions—brief details of their lives that managed to say so much. The fliers said everything, in fact. People stopped to read, but never for long, as grief overcame them. Beneath one photo of a man and his two young daughters was the message, "We love you daddy. Please come home." Another read, "Expecting first child this week." There were details about their clothes, where they were ("Last seen on 100th floor, helping co-workers near elevator bank"), and mention of scars, tattoos, and other distinguishing features.

For weeks and weeks, even after it became obvious that there would be no more rescues at Ground Zero, these signs remained posted around New York. The same faces looked out at us from walls or street lamps or trees, and they became familiar to us—almost like an acquaintance. It wasn't unusual for people to pick out a face among the missing posters and form a secret bond of empathy. Maybe someone their own age who reminded them of themselves. Sometimes the details helped form the bond. Mother of a five-year-old son, perhaps.

One detail that emerged again and again on these fliers was a reference to a certain piece of jewelry many of the missing persons were wearing at the time of this terrible tragedy. "Irish Claddagh ring on left hand." This phrase, and variations of it was listed on countless fliers—a reference to the Irish faith ring with the motto, "Let Love and Friendship Reign." As demographic study of the victims would later show, Irish Americans were heavily represented in those towers on September 11.

Jim Dwyer of the *New York Times*, in an article published on November 11, 2001, estimated that of the nearly 3,000 victims at the World Trade Center, one in five had traces of an Irish background. Dwyer wrote, "Among the surnames of the dead or missing are 12 Lynches, 10 Murphys, 9 Kellys, 5 Egans, 4 McCarthys, multiples of Kennedy, Sullivan, O'Brien, Gallagher. And so on."

In the days following the attack, friends and relatives of the victims filed thousands of missing persons reports with the American Red Cross, and those reports contain numerous mentions of Claddagh rings presumed to have been worn by the missing on that September day. Initial reports about the exact number of Claddagh rings recovered from Ground Zero reached mythic proportions. One such story that has spread across the globe concerns the parents of a missing firefighter who appeared at the site of the World Trade Center rescue operation shortly after the attacks and found the captain in charge of the shift. Perhaps, they told him, their son could be identified by a gold Claddagh ring he had been wearing. The captain, the story goes, had the solemn task of explaining to the heartbroken parents that so far, more than two hundred Claddagh rings had been recovered in the ruins of New York's majestic twin towers.

While people dispute the exact number of Claddagh rings recovered at Ground Zero, the rings do underscore the tragedy. In the days following the attack, Brian Cowen, the Irish foreign minister, appeared in New York to pay respects on behalf of the Irish citizenry. Dwyer reported, in his story in the *New York Times*, that after visiting Ground Zero, a shaken Cowen rode in an elevator at Police Headquarters with a police officer, who explained that in order to identify the missing and dead, family members had been asked to provide a list of personal items—and the Claddagh ring had turned up many times. According to Dwyer, the officer told Cowen that in the police and fire departments alone, "fifteen to twenty of the people we lost were wearing Claddagh rings."

New York's Finest and New York's Bravest, respectively the New York Police and Fire Departments, suffered devastating losses on September 11: twenty-three members of the NYPD, and 343 firemen. Aside from Cantor Fitzgerald, the bond brokerage house that lost 658 employees, the FDNY lost more lives than any other department or company.

Traditionally, Irish Americans have gravitated toward these civil service departments in significant numbers for generations—and fighting New York City fires has long been at the core of the Irish American way of life. In the earliest years of the United States, volunteers formed the corps of firefighting until it became obvious, mostly due to urban development and growth, that full-time firefighters were a necessity. It wasn't until the end of the Civil War that New York City formed a professional firefighting force, which coincided with the boatloads of Irish immigrants who fled genocidal starvation in Ireland and arrived at Ellis Island in tremendous numbers. Because the Irish could speak English, they had an advantage over other groups of immigrants, such as the Germans and the Italians. The Irish had already been making significant political inroads, helping them to secure jobs in public works projects. It did not hurt that some of the bravest soldiers in the Civil War were members of the "Fire Zouaves," a legendary Irish regiment consisting of mostly volunteer firemen from New York City who fought valiantly at Bull Run near Manassas Junction, Virginia, while overwhelmingly outnumbered by Confederate troops. Despite taking hundreds of casualties, the Zouaves withstood a charge by legendary cavalry commander J.E.B. Stuart, and then fell in with another heavily Irish regiment—the 69th from New York. When the Southerners seized the 69th's green regimental flag, the Fire Zouaves advanced into heavy fire and recaptured it.

The earliest New York City firefighters were criminal/political gangs who sometimes fought each other for the privledge of fighting fires. See Herbert Asbury's *Gangs of New York*.

This spirit continued in the early years of the Fire Department of New York, in which the Irish played a major role. Firefighting is perhaps nowhere more dangerous than in New York, where the unofficial motto has been and continues to be, "fight every fire." From 1865 to 1905, one hundred firemen were killed in the line of duty, and two-thirds of those were Irish. Over the years, an influx of new ethnic groups have made the FDNY more representative of the city's diversity, but as evidenced on September 11, 2001, the Irish have still been gravitating to firefighting in heavy numbers.

What is also clear is that the bravery demonstrated by those fighting Zuoaves at Bull Run represents a spirit of heroism and courage that has never wavered in the ranks of the FDNY; and the strength of that legacy reaches across ethnic divides. A hundred firefighters had been killed in action up to September 11. More than 135 years, and one day twice that number were wantonly done to death.

The fact that so many firefighters were wearing Claddagh rings on what turned out to be their last day on earth is proof that what the ring stands for (love, loyalty, and friendship) resonates as strongly now as it has for generations. For the Claddagh ring is no stranger to tragedy, and September 11 was not the first day in history where the hand that wore it met death.

The year was 1845, and the population of Ireland had been growing rapidly over sixty years—exploding to eight million from just three million in the late 1770s. British laws had put a limit on the amount of land Catholics could own, creating smaller plots of land for much of the Irish population to farm. With these small plots, the people relied heavily on the potato crop for subsistence-level farming, and the only way the population could produce enough food on these sub-acre plots was to grow potatoes.

The first signs of a problem appeared in England in the summer of 1845, when a fungus was identified in a potato, leading to a blight. Potato harvests across Europe began to fail, and by fall of that year, the blight had spread to Ireland. A black rot had blanketed the country, destroying any hopes for a bumper crop, and the peasantry found their potatoes rotting in the fields. The economic impact was immediate and devastating, as the people had nothing to pay their British and Protestant landlords for rent. Crop after crop produced no food for six years, and landlords began evicting their tenants. Those who continued to eat the rotten tubers sickened quickly, and before long, entire regions of Ireland grew infested with cholera and typhus.

Thousands upon thousands of peasants underwent removal into workhouses, where they succumbed to disease and starvation. The lucky ones got money from their landlords or through government-sponsored projects to emigrate, and waves of poor and ravaged Irish began to flee in "coffin ships" to America. The poorest, of course, had little choice but to stay behind and accept their fate, and statistically, nowhere was the suffering worse than in western Ireland— particularly Connaught, where the rate of death was five times higher than in many other counties.

Those peasants without the money to set sail for America, often abandoned their land and set off on foot in a desperate search for food, taking other diseases such as typhoid and dysentery with them and spreading them to wider areas of the country. Villages such as Claddagh, the small fishing community in Galway, were able to keep starvation at bay, but they were not able to avoid the cholera that devastated the region.

From 1845 to 1850, over a million lives were lost from starvation and disease, and emigration depleted the population in Ireland to just five million. In 1906, William Dillon, owner of Dillon's, the Galway jeweler, wrote an article entitled "The 'Claddagh' Ring" which appeared in the *Galway Archaeological and Historical Journal*. In the article, Dillon tells a story told to him by a Galway pawnbroker named John Kirwan, who noted that during the Irish famine, people of Claddagh had pawned their gold Claddagh rings for an advance of cash so that they could leave Ireland. Dillon wrote:

> Mr. Kirwan seeing no prospect of them being ever redeemed, realized his money by selling them as old gold to be broken up and consigned to the melting-pot. The 'Claddagh' ring was not at that time the fashionable ring which it is now, and there being no purchasers, these fine old rings, many of them being the rare old G.R. rings now valued for 5 pounds each, were consigned to the melting-pot at the comparatively

low price to be obtained for old gold. The fact is that the Claddagh population was at this time greatly reduced, hundreds going to the USA, where to the present day there exists a colony of them, at Boston, called Claddagh, after their ancestral village.

There is no telling, of course, how many Claddagh rings were displaced from their owners during the Famine. The tradition of passing them down a generation surely continued as people starved or became ill, and as Dillon noted in his story a hundred years ago, all sentimentality vanished in the fight for survival. As the Irish fled the Connemara region where disease and hunger were the most severe, many of them no doubt traveled with Claddagh rings, which, in turn, makes them familiar to oustide people.

Claddagh rings began turning up at Ellis Island during the mass exodus from Ireland in the 19th century, as shiploads of Irish came over with little more than the clothes on their backs. It's realistic to assume, given the numbers of Irish who perished aboard those "coffin ships," that a great many emigrants, with dreams of a better life in America, took their last breath of air with a Claddagh ring upon their finger. These rings were no doubt passed on to relatives and loved ones aboard those ships—in contrast to the tradition mentioned in the poem by Patrick B. Kelly, where a grandmother passes a Claddagh ring to a grateful grandchild. There were no fliers or posters of the faces of the people who perished in the Famine—just the faces of those who survived, and managed to tell a story too tragic and painful for words. Perhaps it's fair to say that only those who lost loved ones in the World Trade Center attacks and had Claddagh rings returned to them can possibly understand the joy and the grief these rings had come to symbolize in a lifetime.

Heartbreak is not, however, a condition commonly associated with the Claddagh ring. Typically there is great joy and ceremony upon the presentation of these rings, as they have, over time, come to represent some of life's happy moments—those of love, friendship, loyalty, and lasting bonds. The history of the Claddagh ring plays a big part, mostly because of the mystery and lore behind it. Those who claim to know the real story simply cannot know the whole story, and the difference between fact and fiction often blurs what is truly known. Yet the remarkable thing is that despite the obvious elements rooted in mythology, the facts that are known about the ring are fascinating with little or no embellishment.

Claddagh rings began turning up at Castle Garden in New York, where millions of immigrants entered the United States before Ellis Island opened in 1892.

The history of the Claddagh ring abounds in mystery and myth, with the result the giver or presenter of this treasure feels as if he or she is involving the beloved recipient in a romantic conspiracy. Each and every one of the givers has a story of the orgins of this symbol with the fact and fiction interwoven so that the real story is never to be known. Does it matter? Well, the real story is as romantic as one can get, so read on!

CHAPTER II

And on her worn hand she told me the story

The Claddagh Ring Stories

A	s is the case with all the great mysteries of the world, the passage of time often clouds memories and recollections, and exaggeration takes the place of fact. Couple that phenomenon with a dose of mythology, and what's left has all the makings of a thoroughly unreliable, though usually enjoyable and entertaining story. Such is the case with the Claddagh ring stories, as they are known—two tales that claim to explain the origins of the Claddagh ring. Both involve the Joyce family of Galway.

Of the two stories, the tale of Margaret Joyce, or "Margaret of the Bridges" as she became known, has always appealed to the most romantic at heart. Margaret lived in sixteenth century Galway, and as fortune would have it, a chance encounter with a Spanish merchant would forever change her life. Not only did she meet the alleged man of her dreams while up to her ankles in water alongside a river-bank where she did the family's laundry, but the man appar-ently fell in love at first sight. And he was quite wealthy. A marriage quickly followed, and so Margaret Joyce soon became Margaret de Rona, wife of Domingo de Rona, who, almost immediately after marrying the young Margaret, whisked her off to Spain on one of his ships. However, the honeymoon would not last long. Domingo was not a young man, and the suddeness of married life may have been a bit too much of a strain on the elderly Spaniard's heart. In short,

Domingo died soon after their return to Spain, and now Margaret de Rona was a young widow with a newly inherited fortune.

Life in Spain, however, did not agree with the homesick Margaret, and after getting her affairs in order, she quickly set sail for Ireland. Too young and too rich to stay a widow for long, Margaret married Oliver Og ffrench, the mayor of Galway, in 1596, and strangely, he set out for a voyage of his own, leaving Margaret at home and apparently restless. Rich and bored are two words that usually do not coincide with significant contributions to mankind. Margaret, however, was inspired to pass the time and spend her money in a manner that the people of western Ireland have greatly appreciated, according to the legend. At her own expense, she began building bridges all over Connaught. It is not clear what her husband, Mayor ffrench, must have thought when he first learned of his wife's little "hobby" while away. Perhaps he didn't mind so much, as this ambitious public works project (which would cost his constituents nothing in taxes!) was sure to help him in his next election campaign. Still, it must have been quite a shock to the French checking account! Countless stone bridges were erected across the Connemara region, with Margaret going from site to site, overseeing much of the work done by masons. Strange as this was, it would only get stranger.

Legend has it that Margaret, while sitting down at one particular bridge project during construction, was visited by a large eagle bearing a gift. In her lap, the eagle dropped the golden prototype of the Claddagh ring as a gift from God for Margaret's charity and good works.

The lore of the eagle dropping the Claddagh ring into the lap of Margaret of the Bridges has captivated many who study the history of Ireland. Historians recount different versions with details varying over time, but the general theme of the tale remains. Hardiman, in his book, *The History of the Town and County of Galway*, written in 1820, wrote of the story of Margaret in great detail:

> Heaven was again propitious to another of this family; Margaret Joyes, great grand daughter of the above named William, who was surnamed, Margaret na Drehide, Margaret of the Bridges, from the great number which she built. The story of this singular woman is still current amongst her descendants. They relate she was born of reduced but genteel parents and was first married to Domingo de Rona, a wealthy Spanish merchant, who traded to Galway, where he fell in love with, and married her; and soon after departing for

Spain, died there, leaving her mistress of an immense property. Upon his decease, having no issue by him, she married Oliver Oge ffrench, who was Mayor of Galway in 1596. So far the narrative is probable and consistent, but what follows will try the credulity of the reader. It relates that this lady, during the absence of her second husband, on a voyage, erected most part of the bridges of the Province of Connaught, at her own expense! And that she was one day sitting before the workmen, when an eagle, flying over her head, let fall into her bosom, a gold ring adorned with a brilliant stone, the nature of which no lapidary could ever discover. It was preserved by her descendants, as a most valuable relique in 1661 (the date of the MS from which this account is taken) as a mark supposed to have been sent from Heaven of its approbation of her good works and charity. This fable though still piously believed, by some of this family, was humorously ridiculed by Latocnaye, an incredulous French traveller, who visited Galway about the end of the last century.

The Frenchman Hardiman referred to was none other than Le Chavalier de la Tocnaye, who traveled around Ireland on a walking tour, and wrote about it in his book, *Promenade d'un francais dans l'Irlande,* published in 1797. In true French fashion, Tocnaye could not help ridiculing the Irish for their fondness for such tales, as is obvious from the following passage from his book:

> It is said also that thirteen families, whose names are still common, laid the city's foundations, and tradition avers that, while a good lady of the name of Joyce watched the masons who built Galway Bridge at her expense, an eagle dropped a chain of gold in her lap, and placed a crown on her head. The gold chain is still preserved by the Joyce family according to the story told to me. The people have always loved fables—had Galway become a Rome this one would certainly have been believed.

It turns out that Tocnaye had a great deal to say about Galway, and not all of it is condescending. But we'll come back to that later. Margaret of the Bridges is the lady who commands our attention at the moment. Nearly 200 years ago, she commanded the attention of one Caesar Otway, author of the book, *A Tour in Connaught*, published in 1839. If Tocnaye demonstrated a bit of skepticism toward the tale of Margaret and her dalliance with the giant bird of prey that came bearing gifts, Otway did the exact opposite. He swallowed the tale, hook-line-and-sinker, and even dared to embellish it, colorfully describing the scene as if he had stumbled into the stream himself, and with paper and pen, recorded the events for all the world to enjoy.

Tocnaye wrote that Margaret, the daughter of John Joyce, was out one day washing clothes in a stream off the River Corrib, when who should gallantly ride by but Don Domingo de Rona, the wealthy Biscayan merchant. De Rona had come to Galway with "a barrack" of Benecarlo wine, an ingredient in high demand by the local merchants who were famous for "doctoring the claret" with their own custom concoctions. Tocnaye describes Margaret working away in the stream with toes "as straight and fair as her fingers, not a corn or bunnion on one of them" as she washed the family linen. "The don," he wrote, "was captivated with the maid; he made love as Spaniards do; produced proofs of his pedigree, and his cash, and in due time they were married, and proceeded to Corunna."

However, not long after the marriage, de Rona died (for he was no spring chicken at the time of his dalliances with fair Margaret), and "Donnade Rona" came back to Ireland a "sparkling and wealthy widow." De la Tocnaye noted that one Oliver Og ffrench took a liking to Margaret upon her return, and after a more lengthy courtship, the two eventually married.

Ffrench then became mayor of Galway and one of the most successful merchants in the city—and was not above engaging himself in the popular Galway tradition of smuggling restricted goods overseas. Meanwhile, Margaret, a.k.a. Donna Domingo de Rona ffrench by this time, was idle by no means. De la Tocnaye then describes the sequence of events as she set out to become the "greatest improver in the west" by engaging in her passion for building bridges:

> She might have made as good a pontifex at Pope Joan, and heaven's blessing was on her for her good works; for one day as she was superintending her masons, an eagle came soaring from the ocean, and balancing itself with poised wing just over the dame, it dropped at her feet a ring formed of a single stone, so strange and outlandish in its make and form, but yet so beautiful and so precious that, though the most skilful lapidarires admired it, and would have given any price for it, none could say of what kind it was, or

of what country or age was the workmanship; it has been kept in the family since. I wish I could tell the reader which of the Joyces now owns this precious relic. All I can say is, that it is not on the finger of big Jack, or his wife. But indeed the Joyces seem to have been a favoured race; it is a favour that they should be named and known as merry; for he who has 'a merry hath a continual feast'. I assume it to be a favour also that they were under the especial patronage of eagles.

Whether a crown was also placed on Margaret's head, or a "brilliant stone" placed in her lap, or whether she simply received the prototype of the Claddagh ring itself as a gift for her good works, is a detail that depends on the story-teller. In most versions, however, the design of the Claddagh ring was preserved by the Joyce family from 1661, thanks to the eagle and Margaret's passion for bridge building. Realistically, many of the elements of the Margaret story are rooted in Greek mythology, folklore, and fairytales common throughout Europe.

For instance, the great Greek dramatist, Aeschylus (525–456 B.C.), author of *Prometheus Bound* and *Oresteia* and widely considered the father of Greek tragedy, was also inextricably (and tragically) linked to the giant bird. Not only did Aquila the eagle play an important part in *Prometheus Bound*, meting out Zeus's punishment by continually swooping down on Prometheus each dawn, pecking at his liver, but Aeschylus found himself at the mercy of such a bird. Lore has it that an eagle, soaring overhead, mistook Aeschylus's head for a stone, and dropped a tortoise on it, killing the dramatist instantly.

It is possible that Tocnaye, in his sarcastic gibe about Margaret's eagle, may have had another eagle from ancient Rome in mind. The legend goes that Roman engineers were surveying plans to make ancient Troy the capital of the Eastern Empire. Suddenly, an eagle swooped down and seized the measuring line from the engineers, dropping it in Byzantium, thereby redefining the capital.

Margaret Joyce, a.k.a. Margaret de Rona, a.k.a. Margaret French, a.k.a. Margaret of the Bridges, has been depicted in countless paintings and portrayed in numerous stories pertaining to the mysteries of the Claddagh ring's origin. Whether or not a swooping eagle descended from the skies over Connaught to bestow a ring, a stone, and a crown upon the head of fair Margaret is not at issue here. Rather, the allure and the mystery of the tale is almost secondary to how it, and the design of the Claddagh ring, were preserved in a tiny, secluded fishing village in County Galway for so many years. For the history of the village of Claddagh is every bit as intriguing as how Margaret of the Bridges came to hold the secret of the Claddagh design.

Not as mystical, but just as intriguing, is the tale of Richard Joyce, who holds the key to the second story of the origin of the ring.

RICHARD JOYCE

In truth, the saga of Richard Joyce is, in many ways, every bit as romantic and mysterious as the story of Margaret of the Bridges. But because Richard's story does not feature any supernatural occurrences (such as Margaret's eagle delivering precious jewelry), many owners of Claddagh rings are inclined to believe that Richard's story is more in line with the origins of the Claddagh design. While it is true that his saga boasts more than its fair share of intrigue and adventure and is more plausible than the tale of Margaret Joyce, not everyone who owns a Claddagh ring can be sure that Richard's hands pounded out the very first Claddagh ring. With that said, there is no disputing the fact that Richard Joyce, also referred to as Richard "Joyes," was a master goldsmith, and many of the earliest Claddagh rings in existence, dating back some three hundred years or so, bear his initials and his jeweler's mark.

In 1675, Richard Joyce, a native of Galway, was on his way to the West Indies, presumably aboard some type of merchant vessel. Adding to the usual danger of a sea voyage in those days was the constant threat of pirate ships. Corsairs, under Ottoman protection, dominated the Mediterranean seas, most notably along waters of North Africa, known as the "Barbary Coast." Manning these ships were Muslim pirates from Algeria, Morocco, Tunisia, and other states, authorized by their government to raid and plunder commercial ships trading with Christian countries. They disrupted trade in the region so skillfully that even Great Britain, with the world's most powerful navy, could not stop them. In fact, the Corsairs had begun to expand operations to the Atlantic, and were known to attack ships and towns from the Caribbean to the uppermost parts of North America.

Unfortunately for Richard Joyce, the pirates who raided his vessel were not only interested in the typical pirate booty of currency, food, and whatever else a ship might contain. The Algerian privateers were noted for capturing and enslaving passengers from these vessels. Some of them were sold, others transported and enslaved in Algeria. For almost fifteen years, until his release in 1689, Richard Joyce was a captive in Algeria, purchased by a successful Turkish goldsmith. It was during this time that Joyce apparently learned and mastered the craft that would ultimately gain him considerable wealth.

Once again, James Hardiman, in his book, *The History of the Town and County of Galway* (1820), describes Joyce's ordeal and release in the following manner:

> Several individuals of this name have long felt grateful to the memory of William III, from the following circumstance, on the accession of that monarch to the throne of England. One of the first acts of his reign was to send an ambassador to Algiers, to demand the immediate release of all the British subjects detained there in slavery. The dey and council, intimidated, reluctantly complied with this demand. Among those released was a young man of the name of Joyes, a native of Galway, who fourteen years before, was captured on his passage to the West Indies, by an Algerine Corsair; on his arrival at Algiers, he was purchased by a wealthy Turk who followed the profession of a goldsmith, and who observing his slave, Joyes, to be tractable and ingenious, instructed him in his trade in which he speedily became an adept. The Moor, as soon as he heard of his release, offered him, in case he should remain, his

only daughter in marriage, and with her half
his property, but all these, with other tempt-
ing and advantageous proposals, Joyes reso-
lutely declined.

Joyce returned to Galway, married, and ultimately became
one of Ireland's most renowned goldsmiths. He brought back
to Ireland not only a skill honed abroad (albeit in some try-
ing circumstances), but also a style that was unique to the
country and steeped in Moorish influence. He produced
many silver chalices and other artifacts in this vein, but it was
his rings, with the heart, the hands, and the crown that captured the imagination of generations. Fortunately, many of
the rings Joyce produced upon returning from Algeria survive today and bear his initials and marks. These are the oldest known Claddagh rings in existence, and are no doubt the
reason so many are willing to believe that the origin of the
Claddagh ring's design can be attributed to Richard Joyce—
the young man captured by Algerian Corsairs, and put to
work by a master goldsmith.

While the tale of Margaret Joyce and her acquisition of
the Claddagh ring is romantic enough to endure over the
years, her story pretty much ends at the bridge after the visit
by the eagle. Richard Joyce, on the other hand, continues to
be a focal point for historians, as more details emerge of his

work with Claddagh rings in Galway. What is most fascinating about his story is how a tiny and mysterious fishing village made the ring its own after Joyce stopped producing them circa 1737. The history of this peaceful community along Galway Bay only adds to the allure, the charm, and the mystery of the Claddagh ring.

CHAPTER III

It was made where the Claddagh rolls
down to the sea

The Village of Claddagh

THE CLADDAGH BOATMAN

by Dr. Jeremiah Dowling

(1830–1906)

I am a Claddagh boatman bold,
Quite humble is my calling,
From morn 'til night,
From dark 'til light,
Round Galway Bay I'm trawling.

I care not for the great man's frown,
I ask not for his favour,
My wants are few,
No debts I've due,
I live by honest labour.

I have one son a gallant boy,
Not stained by spot, nor speckle,
He pulls and hauls
And works the trawls,
And keeps right trim the tackle.

His father trained his son to be,
Hard working, honest, manly,
The sagart says round Galway Bay,
There's none like young Matt Hanley.

I have thank God a girl as good,
Dear Eileen, slight and slender,
She works and mends,
And brightens home
With love that's bright and tender.

When Sunday brings that hour of rest,
That sweet relief from labour,
We crossed the fields in friendly groups,
And gossiped with our neighbors.

We and they, put in the day,
With harmless recreation
Could Erin's sons live their lives
And need no emigration.

This much is true so far—Richard Joyce was making Claddagh rings in Galway in the late 17th century and early 18th century, and rings bearing his initials and jeweler's markings prove it. In fact, he designed the earliest known Claddagh rings. Whether or not we accept the story of him being captured by Algerian corsairs, learning the goldsmith's trade while in captivity, and ultimately becoming so skilled in the craft that his wealthy Turkish master offered a daughter's hand in marriage so that he would not return to Ireland, is beside the point. Perhaps he caught a glimpse of the design from a relative of Margaret of the Bridges, who, just a century earlier, had received a Claddagh ring as a gift from an eagle! The mystery of the ring's origin will no doubt remain just that—a mystery for the ages.

Yet we do know that after Richard Joyce retired from manufacturing Claddagh rings around 1737, interest in the ring had waned severely for a more than a generation. In fact, the ring may have disappeared forever were it not for the customs and idiosyncrasies of a tiny, ancient village in Galway—a unique village that refused to be part of or governed by the powers that be in Galway, and that was governed by its own King—the King of the Claddagh. There are many myths surrounding the village of Claddagh, simply because the Claddagh was a community that kept to itself. Suspicious of outsiders, and extraordinarily insular and protective, the people of Claddagh did nothing to remove the cloak of mystery that enveloped the sleepy village on Galway Bay. Yet this is precisely the reason the Claddagh rings live on today. They have become, in a sense, a lasting reminder of a people that has slowly disappeared from the land.

Yet the strangers came and tried to teach us their ways,
They scorned us for being what we are.

But they might as well go chasing after moonbeams,
Or light a penny candle from a star.

Galway Bay by Arthur Colahan

THE OLD CLADDAGH

Archeologists can give us only estimates of when the area known as "The Claddagh" saw its first settlers. Stone axe blades discovered along the banks of the River Corrib some six thousand years ago (4,000 B.C.) suggest that Mesolithic people had discovered the rich hunting and fishing in the area during the Stone Age. Seafood was abundant in the shallow waters off Mutton Island, and these early settlers no doubt realized this extraordinarily rich environment was not one to stray from. They farmed the lands along the River Corrib, and for thousands of years, Claddagh appears to have been a busy and thriving fishing community.

By the ninth century, Vikings were coming down to Ireland in waves, and they did not come bearing gifts. They ravaged the entire province of Connaught, yet they mysteriously chose other places in Ireland to settle, like Limerick and Dublin. It is not entirely clear why the Vikings found Galway to be too remote to settle, but they eventually all but abandoned the area, leaving it to the local tribes to wage war over. James Hardiman noted that the Irish, once the Danes had gone, worked diligently at rebuilding Galway, which had been in an absolute state of disrepair and home to mostly fishermen families.

As they rebuilt, suspicion arose as to their intent, especially upon the construction of the castle of Galway, and it wasn't long before Conor, the king of Munster, in 1132, sent commander Cormac McCarthy with an army to destroy the castle before its completion, insuring that a formidable fort would not be placed in such a strategic location. This pattern was repeated time and time again, over decades, in fact, until a new conquering force arrived in Ireland—one that would not relinquish its desire to hold Galway. The Norman conquest was immediate, and it has had a lasting effect on Irish culture.

Unlike the Vikings, the Normans immediately recognized the beauty and potential of the lush region alongside Galway Bay. Descendants of Vikings themselves who had settled in France, and the greatest conquerors in medieval Europe, the Normans descended on Galway in the early 12th century. They fast defeated local tribes and began to fortify the town, making Galway their own by erecting a protective wall and buildings of stone. They drove the Irish out of town, securing their own occupation within the confines of the stone-fortified city.

Taking part in the invasion was a powerful family known as the "de-Burgos" who, under the direction of Henry II of England, took land from the local tribes and paved the way for more Norman families to arrive in the region and stake their own claim. Fourteen families, according to Hardiman, bore these surnames (Athy, Blake, Bodkin, Browne, D'Arcy, Deane, Ffont, ffrench, Joyes, Kirwan, Lynch, Martin, Morris, and Skerrett).

These families, recognizing the value of the land in a way the Vikings did not, established a tremendously profitable seaport, gaining much power and wealth in the process. They soon formed a government of their own—one that would last for the next two centuries, after a charter was granted to them in 1484 from Richard III. These tribes were most loyal to England, but were also highly autonomous because of England's involvement in war, yet this would create something of a rift later on, as the tribes would also become devoted Catholics. Just outside the walls of Galway, a small village known as Claddagh prospered.

It is the Joyce family that is of particular interest to our story.

The first Joyce to arrive in Ireland was Thomas de Jorse, who was actually of Welsh descent. De Jorse is said to have arrived in 1282 in Thomond, Ireland, and the following year, he married Nora O'Brien, the daughter of the Prince of Thomond. The newlyweds returned to sea and sailed for

Galway or at least "Iar Connacht" (West Connaught), and after Nora gave birth to a son on the ship (named Edmond "MacMara" meaning "son of the sea"), they arrived and stayed in County Mayo temporarily before finally making it to the northwestern part of Galway. De Jorse formed an alliance with the powerful O'Flaherty family, chiefs of West Connaught (Edmond would later marry into the family), and was able to acquire a great deal of land in Connemara—a part of Ireland that would become known as "Joyce Country."

The Joyce family, over generations, proved to be an honorable, brave, and noble family, engaging in numerous tribal battles in the region, most notably in battles with the Bourke family from a region north of Connemara. In fact, the Joyce clan motto is *mors aut honorabilis vita* (death, or life with honor). The Joyces waged war with Tioboid na Luinge (Theobald of the ships), and as a result of their victory, the Joyces claimed a good-sized portion of Bourke land. They also did battle with the O'Flahertys, ironically over land formally given to Edmond as dowry, but the Joyces were able to defend against their enemies with great success.

Despite the fact that Cromwellian forces were able to confiscate land from the Joyce family more effectively than other tribes, the Joyces were able to maintain extensive landholdings in the region, and "Joyce's Country" is still today printed on maps of Ireland. And while Richard Joyce might be the most relevant and noted "Joyce" in this book, it is another Joyce—this one by the name of James, born in 1882 in Dublin and author of some of the greatest novels in the English language—who is the most familiar Joyce of Irish descent.

Still, despite their ability to hold and control a large portion of the west of Ireland, there was one part of the region that remained virtually untouched.

Claddagh, or *An Claddach*, as it is known in Irish, meaning "stony shore," over the next few centuries, would establish itself as the most important fishing village on the west coast of Ireland. It remained an Irish-speaking village, independent of Norman rule in Galway during the Middle Ages, and as the city of Galway began to grow, Claddagh could not be more distant in terms of customs, traditions, and way of life. Fishing defined the village, and fishermen and their families rose to a position of great respect in the community. Cod and herring were fished in prodigious amounts and the Claddagh fisherman were the largest suppliers in the land.

The Dominican fathers came to Claddagh in 1488, and despite several expulsions by Cromwellian forces over the years, they formed a strong and lasting relationship with the Claddagh community, erecting and re-erecting St. Mary's on the Hill—a church which, after several rebuilding projects, still stands in Claddagh. After the Dominicans established churches, the Claddagh people began building thatched houses near the places of worship, and the village began to grow. Still, by 1695, it was estimated that there were just a little over five hundred people living in Claddagh.

Information supplied to the Irish House of Commons in 1762 stated that almost two hundred boats from Galway were fishing the bay, and historians are quick to add that they were nearly all from Claddagh. The area remained heavily fished and was part of the Whaley estate, land granted to a Cromwellian army officer by the name of Colonel Whaley. It was at this time that the penal laws were in force and could be summed up in one verse. Catholics could not read nor teach, plead nor preach, and the Dominicans were often forced to abandon their places of worship in Claddagh. The Galway Corporation began imposing taxes on fish the Claddagh men had brought into town, which was significant because Claddagh was supplying fish along the west coast and into the midlands of Ireland.

The success these fishermen had in the bay brought more people into the village, and by 1812, the population there had approached 3,000, with over 2,000 fishermen living in Claddagh. Thatch-roofed homes with whitewashed walls had sprung up in "clachans," which were jagged rows of farmhouses built one next to the other. In his book *In Search of Ireland* (1930), H.V. Morton gave the following description of the clachans.

Nothing is more picturesque in the British Isles than this astonishing fishing village of neat, whitewashed, thatched cottages planted at haphazard angles with no regular roads running to them. If you took three hundred little toy cottages and jumbled them up on a nursery floor, you would have something like the Claddagh. It is a triumph of unconscious beauty.

The steady rains and unsteadying winds blew and sprayed the dirt roads so that these thatched homes were often spattered with mud, appearing to visitors as though the inhabitants lived in squalor. In fact, Claddagh was a curious place for many outsiders. Often, they found what they perceived to be filthy living conditions, and this perception lingered for centuries, well past the years of the Famine. Yet some visitors, such as Richard Lovett, the author who traveled around Ireland in the late 19th century and wrote about the country in his book, *Irish Pictures* (1888), noted that little had changed over time in Claddagh. Lovett was able to shed light on an important detail of life that few who merely observed the village from a distance could comprehend. Lovett wrote:

The appearance of the village of the Claddagh is dirty, but the houses are clean enough inside;

and be it known that before the famine their houses were models of cleanliness; and we must recollect that those manure heaps which frequently offend the eye in Irish villages have no offensive odour, on account of the deodorizing power of the peat which forms a large portion of the compost. The men and women have generally clean linen, although often covered with rags. It is a general fact worthy of note that in Ireland a dirty outside generally covers a clean heart.

The Claddagh Lovett observed from his travels was not much different from Claddagh a century before. Many of the streets were made of cobblestone instead of dirt, which went a long way toward sprucing up the appearance of the village and also solved some drainage problems the dung heaps had caused. But all in all, the village was perceived by most who saw it before the 20th century as a land that time forgot. This was possible because Claddagh had a purpose. They were fishermen and they had work to do.

Much has been written about this mysterious and secluded seaside town that once captured the imagination of the European traveler when he read of its odd and secretive customs. In 1860, Julius Rodenberg wrote an account of his travels throughout Ireland (*The Island of Saints*, 1861), and some historians consider his description of Claddagh to be among the most relevant observations of the small fishing village outside of Galway. It is not known how long Rodenberg visited Claddagh, but it is obvious from his description that he did gain some insights beyond what most travel writers up to this date had been able to gather. He went on to write a colorful and highly detailed account of the town that had long been an enigma, even to the people of Ireland. Rodenberg saw Galway itself as a land of legends and folklore, with customs that were unique to Ireland. He called to mind the influence of the Spanish, especially the Spanish Arch—a remnant of centuries gone by, and most remarkable to him were the women who gathered there to sell their wares. He wrote:

> The market in front was full of blue cloak, lying behind the casks and selling shell-fish, and of red petticoats, walking among them. The younger women, with the cloaks draped round their heads, looked often piquant enough; their faces had not unfrequently the sweetest expression of passion, and their lips pouted charmingly. The old fisher-wives, on the other hand, who sat near the casks and

smoked damp tobacco in short clay pipes, had something witch-like and menacing about them.

Rodenberg noted that he did not hear any English spoken at the market. The buyers were from the country, and the women from Claddagh were "nothing but Irish blood." He learned that the men of this village fulfilled their duties by fishing the bay with a diligence and dedication that called to mind a tradition and way of life that appeared to have changed little over the centuries. Yet when they returned from sea, Rodenberg wrote, they became the "lazzaroni of the West," lounging about while their women went to market with their catch:

> These cabin aristocrats do not trouble them-selves with trade. The rotting boat, the crumbling cabin are their abode—everything else they despise. They call every man who does not belong to their community a stranger.

Rodenberg learned that the Claddagh men had appeared untouched from the famine and disease that plagued the land not long before he observed them. They had resisted every influence they came into contact with after centuries of invasions by the Danes, Saxons, and Normans, and did not mix with the Spanish either. During his visit, Rodenberg also witnessed the "Blessing of the Bay" as well as the commencement of a Claddagh King's reign and the bonfire celebration and costumed dance that began the ceremony.

The Claddagh names were a curious thing to Rodenberg, who noted they were "thoroughly Irish." Many in the village had the same name, and so they were differentiated by a manner usually associated with a fish, such as "Paddy the Salmon," "Paddy the Whale," and "Paddy the sprout." He also found that despite the fact that these men could indeed speak English, they would never, among themselves, make use of a "Sassenach" (Saxon) word.

Rodenberg was also fascinated with the Irish love of colorful clothing. The short blue cloaks worn by the Claddagh women were of particular interest to him, as were the red petticoats and handkerchiefs worn around their heads. As far as the men were concerned, Rodenberg observed that the fisherman of the Claddagh were the bravest he'd ever seen at sea, yet on land they were often "retiring and timid"—and "cannot endure the sight of fire-arms, and are no hands at boxing."

It is Rodenberg's last observation, regarding the Claddagh fishermen's timidity, that makes one wonder about the legendary nature of their behavior at sea when encountering a non-Claddagh fishing boat in the waters of the Bay. In fact, it's difficult to imagine men who don't like to fight and who cringe at the sight of firearms on land, suddenly becoming ruthless killers at the sight of another boat. Still, the mysterious and secretive society that was the Claddagh must have brought fear into the hearts of non-complying fishermen at the sight of the Claddagh boats heading their way.

GALWAY HOOKERS

Galway might be the only city in the world where you can walk up to a group of policemen (*gardai*), and get not so much as a raised eyebrow if you ask, "Where can I find some old hookers?" Okay, maybe Amsterdam, too. But the reason the *gardai* would not blink at your question is because everyone in Galway knows that "hookers" are old fishing boats, and the men of the Claddagh used hookers and smaller variations of these boats to fish the waters of the bay.

The waters of Galway Bay are treacherous for small boats. The bay is wide open, and the Aran Islands did little to protect fishermen from sudden storms that often blew in with very little warning. The hookers did not venture deep into the Atlantic; rather their sailors choose to work the shores along Connemara. Because the Atlantic storms might rage at a moment's notice, the Claddagh men would have to dart their hookers inland for safety, so the boats were never more than an hour or so away from land.

Most of the Claddagh boats were small, usually between 24 and 32 feet long, and they were distinct in the waters of Galway Bay because of their three brown sails. Mary Banim, in her book, *Here and There Through Ireland* (1892), described them as:

> . . . Very old fashioned boats, but of a most graceful build—the keel sharp as a razor, the ribs—or "knees" as a fisherboy told me to call the sides—bowed out almost in the shape of the breast-bone of a water fowl, then sloped in again to the edge of the vessel; the bow, rising high out of the water, and curving up a little in front, gives a picturesque appearance to the boat, which seems to ride on the waves with the ease and buoyancy of a bird. The fishermen say that the bowing out of the "knees" gives greater steadiness and security: certainly the vessel can go through the water at a flying speed.

Once the Claddagh men departed from the quays, they would fish mostly with nets for cod and herring, but line fishing was also common. Historians have noted that the Claddagh men used rather primitive fishing techniques in relation to European counterparts of the same era. Their nets were often heavier and required constant maintenance by the Claddagh men and women once they returned to shore, and the entire community was involved in the details of fishing. Nets and lines were stretched and laid out for mending across an area known as the "Big Grass," and women and children could also be seen along the strands before the men went off to fish, collecting worms and other bait.

Author James Hardiman, in his book, *The History of the Town and County of Galway*, noted the Claddagh's steadfast refusal to modernize its techniques, even if it meant less productive catches and more labor. He observed that the people of the village "exhibit a great shew of industry." They absolutely reject, "with the most inveterate prejudice," making use of technological advances and improvements in their fishing equipment—improvements far superior to the centuries-old equipment that their ancestors used. The effect, Hardiman wrote, was that the great wealth of resources in the bay had hardly been tapped, and the Claddagh fisherman had only "partially explored" the region's potential.

The reason, Hardiman concluded, was their indolence, as well as the "superstitious prejudices of this otherwise useful and meritorious body of men." Hardiman could not understand how, "when they do not themselves think proper to fish, they invariably prevent any other from attempting it, viewing with all the monopolizing spirit of any corporation, the bay as their exclusive domain, on which to use their own words, they never admit any trespesser; and, therefore, should a single boat from any other district venture out to fish, without the concurrence of the Claddagh body, it does so at the risk of being destroyed."

That the Claddagh boats laid claim to all rights to fish the bay, and were fiercely protective of their waters, is not surprising. To outsiders, however, it made little sense that on certain days, there would be no boats out at all, yet the Claddagh men refused to allow a single boat to fish the bay. Hardiman hinted at the danger other fisherman faced should they venture out to Galway Bay without permission from Claddagh, but to what extent the Claddagh men protected their rights to the waters has been a matter of speculation for centuries. Lore had it that if the Claddagh men came upon another boat in the bay, and it did not display the Claddagh symbol, everyone aboard the vessel would be killed. Other tales told of hungry men attempting to fish the bay during one of Claddagh's self-imposed "non-fishing days," and suddenly finding themselves sailing for their lives as the angry Claddagh boats approached.

While there were certain to have been confrontations on those waters, and some probably led to violence, the notion of blood-thirsty Claddagh men on the hunt for boats in the bay without Claddagh symbols seems far-fetched. Yet it was a legend and myth that worked in the best interests of the Claddagh fishermen. The village was mysterious enough to most, and the odd men who fished those waters certainly had a serious look about them. Why take the chance to find out if they were as violent as legend had it? These were the same men who, if they spotted a red-haired woman or saw a rabbit or even heard mention of the name, would not set sail that day. And so, the prevailing notion of the day was to avoid completely the dark brown sails of the Claddagh hookers.

BLESSING OF THE BAY

The truth was that the Claddagh village was quite peaceful, and the people were deeply religious. But like most seafaring folk, they were superstitious when it came to fishing. The unpredictable nature of fishing itself led to various customs or traditions performed before a trip for good luck, such as burying a cat in the hopes of favorable winds, or not playing any music on the boats for fear of a poor catch. But toward the end of the 18th century, many of these superstitions faded, and by 1835, to appeal to God for a bountiful season, a Dominican Father would lead the Claddagh boats out to what would become the annual Blessing of the Bay.

The special ceremony took place each August at the start of the herring season. Hundreds of Claddagh boats headed out to the bay, with the priest in the bow, stopping at an area near Mutton Island, where the Dominican Father recited prayers. Mary Banim, in her book, *Here and There Through Ireland*, gave this account:

> When all were in place the king stood up, took off his hat and waved it. In one instant, every human being in the fleet was bareheaded and on his knees, and the prayer began. First the Rosary and Litany were recited, and oh! what deep faith and devotion, what earnest, imploring petitions were in the voices and in the gravely attentive faces of those men! The priest, used to touching scenes, could scarcely master his emotions as he sent up fervent prayers for God's blessing on the poor fishermen around him, while the responses of the soft, childish voices beside us mingled sweetly with the men's deep, earnest tones, coming like a chorus over the waters. The Rosary and Litany ended, the priest arose from his knees and read the service for the occasion, and, sprinkling the waves three

times with holy water, he implored a blessing on them in the name of the Father, Son, and Holy Ghost.

What Mary Banim witnessed toward the end of the 19th century was surely not much different from the Blessing of the Bay some two generations before in Galway Bay. The custom continues to this day, but it is more ceremonial in nature as a remembrance of the cultural forces that shaped the city long ago. Banim also mentioned that this ceremony could commence only when a man stood up and waved his hat, signaling the beginning of the Blessing. In stark contrast to the brown-sailed hookers of the day, the man with the hat would take to the water in a boat with white sails—indication that he was none other than the admiral, mayor, and King of the Claddagh.

KING OF THE CLADDAGH

Not much is known about the precise role of the King of the Claddagh in earlier times, but from certain customs and rituals that have been documented, we do know that his presence in the village was far more practical than ceremonial. The Claddagh King was usually a well-respected fisherman in the village who did not stand out amongst the other fishermen in the bay except for the white sails on his mast, and he was responsible for upholding rules and traditions both at sea and on land. He did not sit back and rule Claddagh by collecting taxes or live in a more palatial dwelling. He was a regular fisherman most times, which was part of the appeal of his title.

But aside from signaling the start of the Blessing of the Bay, it was often the King who decided on which days fishing would take place, and he no doubt settled any disputes that arose in the community, since the inhabitants were not very likely to seek outside intervention. The Claddagh people were also more inclined to accept punishment from him, rather than allow police into what they perceived as private matters in Claddagh. Anna and Samuel Hall wrote *Handbooks for Ireland: The West and Connamara* (1853) and gained a unique insight into life in Claddagh during their travels. It was their thought that the Claddagh King was more mayor than royalty:

> He has still, however, much influence, and sacrifices himself, literally without fee or reward, for "the good of the people;" he is constantly occupied hearing and deciding causes and quarrels, for his people never, by any chance, appeal to a higher tribunal.

There were, no doubt, some responsibilities on the part of the King to help insure that the Claddagh way of life continued, and because people did not marry and leave the village, it was probably not unusual for the King to have a say in marital issues.

CLADDAGH RING MARRIAGES

In his book, *Down by the Claddagh* (1993), the noted Galway historian Peadar O'Dowd described scenes from a typical Claddagh festivity centuries ago, where people gathered around bonfires. Then, a young man pulled a lighted stick from the fire and tossed it in the direction of the girl he desired. If the girl picked up the stick and threw it back at the boy, they were a match, and marriage would follow soon afterward. O'Dowd notes that these couples were quite young, but that in Claddagh tradition, marriage was for life, and separation or adultery was unheard of in the village. Hardiman clearly had the pleasure of witnessing one of these ceremonies and gained some insights into the Claddagh marriages of the late 18th and early 19th centuries:

> A marriage is commonly preceded by an
> elopement; but no disappointment or dishon-

orable advantage, arising from that circumstance has ever been known among them. A reconciliation between the young couple and their respective friends generally takes place the morning after the elopement; the clergyman's part of the ceremony is then performed, and the nuptials are solemnized with a boisterous kind of merriment usual only on these occasions. A cabin is soon provided for the new-married pair, who now, in their turn, commence housekeeping. The parents, if in good circumstances, contrive to supply the price of a boat (or at least a share in one) for the husband, and this, with a few articles of furniture, commonly constitute the entire of their worldly possessions.

The people of Claddagh lived very simply and did not own much beyond what they needed to survive. Money was spent on furnishings, clothes, food, fishing supplies, and repairs. The women of Claddagh usually managed a family's finances, selling the fish from a day's catch and spending the money as frugally as possible. It was common in Claddagh for the woman to give what amounted to an allowance to her husband when he returned from a trip and the fish were sold.

A small amount to buy a few pints and tobacco for their pipes. Hardiman noted:

> The women possess unlimited control over their husbands, the produce of whose labours they exclusively manage, allowing the men little more money than suffice to keep their boats in repair, but they have the policy, at the same time, to keep them plentifully supplied with their usual luxuries, whiskey, brandy and tobacco, of which they themselves also liberally partake.

Many who observed life in Claddagh believed that the men were simply more comfortable at sea than they were on land, and that the women had a better understanding of the social and financial norms that dictated commerce. The men, it was felt, needed all their strength for fishing, and it was best to keep them happy and not troubled by the daily goings on of village life.

Aside from the investment in a decent fishing boat, the people of Claddagh had another expensive object they were willing to spend money on—the piece of jewelry that would eventually become known as the Claddagh ring. These rings were often commissioned in Galway by Claddagh families, who would pay as much as a few pounds for one—a fortune in those days for a fisherman's family. How much money they could spend determined just how large and how much gold would go into the ring.

As Patrick B. Kelly wrote in his old song and poem, "Old Claddagh Ring," the rings would remain in the village for generations as a family heirloom. Anna and Samuel Hall noted the method by which the rings were presented at Claddagh weddings:

> The wedding ring is an heir-loom in a family. It is regularly transferred by the mother to her daughter first married; and so on to their descendants. The rings are large, of solid gold, and not unfrequently cost from two to three pounds each.

Yet there are also accounts that the rings were passed from grandmother to first married granddaughter, who would present the ring to her fiancé, only to have it returned to his bride after the wedding ceremony. This would mean that the mother of the bride would keep her own Claddagh ring and present it to her first granddaughter years down the road. Whichever was the case, and it was likely that the custom simply evolved over time, it was certain that the tradition of presenting a Claddagh ring to a loved one remained consistent, and it was the Old Claddagh that kept this tradition alive at a time when Claddagh rings had all but disappeared.

Ida Delamer, in an article published in the *Irish Arts Review Yearbook* (1996), reported that of the existing Claddagh rings made before 1840, none were small enough to be considered a woman's ring. This fact adds an interesting wrinkle to the mystery of the Claddagh rings. Would the Claddagh fishermen, whose wives often controlled their money, commission expensive rings for themselves, when they spent the bulk of their time pulling and throwing nets in Galway Bay? If so, it is certain the rings were kept at home. Delamer also felt that the people of Claddagh could not afford to pay for solid gold rings, and therefore, obtained rings made of other materials, such as bronze or lesser fine gold.

Yet the mystery may forever remain just that. The Claddagh people endured some dreadful privations, especially during the Great Hunger, which killed many and sent millions fleeing to the United States. Claddagh rings were often pawned and melted down to pay for transport or debt, and as Sean McMahon points out in his book, *The Story of the Claddagh Ring* (1999), it may just be that the rings Delamer examined for her article simply did not come from Claddagh, but from wealthy people who commissioned them, and who did not have to worry about pawning them to survive.

Folklore, it would seem, has embellished the role of the rings in the Claddagh way of life. It was, perhaps, just happenstance that these fede rings came to symbolize life, friendship, love, and tradition in a quaint village on Galway Bay. Yet there can be no denying that these rings meant a great deal to the people of Claddagh, and the beautiful simplicity of their lives and values will be forever represented in the ring that bears the name of their village.

CHAPTER IV

'Twas true love entwined in the old Claddagh ring

Let Love and Friendship Reign

T O UNDERSTAND JUST how the Claddagh ring may have developed, whether or not you choose to believe either of the romantic stories of Margaret and Richard, it is important to understand the origins of rings and the purposes for wearing them. In his book, *Rings for the Finger* (J.B. Lippincott Company, 1917), author George Frederick Kunz explains some of the earliest recognition of the ring as a bonding symbol:

> The origin of the ring is somewhat obscure, although there is good reason to believe that it is a modification of the cylindrical seal which was first worn attached to the neck or to the arm and was eventually reduced in size so that it could be worn on the finger.
>
> . . . In his *Natural History*, Pliny related the Greek fable of the origin of the ring. For his impious daring in stealing fire from heaven for mortal man, Prometheus had been doomed by Jupiter to be chained for 30,000 years to a rock in the Caucasus, while a vulture fed upon his liver. Before long, however, Jupiter relented and liberated Prometheus; nevertheless, in order to avoid a violation of the original judgment, it was

ordained that the Titan should wear a link of his chain on one of his fingers as a ring, and in this ring was set a fragment of the rock to which he had been chained, so that he might be still regarded as bound to the Caucasian knot.

It is interesting that Kunz mentions the knot as these were known for being an early favorite charm in primitive times—a piece of knotted cord or wire would be twisted into a knot. Kunz continues:

Frequently this was used to cast a spell over a person, so as to deprive him of the use of one of his limbs or one of his faculties: at other times, the power of the charm was directed against the evil spirit which was supposed to cause disease or lameness, and in this case the charm had curative power. It has been conjectured that the magic virtues attributed to rings originated in this way, the ring being regarded as a simplified form of a knot; indeed, not infrequently rings were and are made in the form of knots. This symbol undoubtedly signified the binding or attach-

ing of the spell to its object, and the same idea
is present in the true-lovers' knot.

If the origins of the Claddagh ring are swathed in intrigue,
mystery, and folklore, the meaning of the ring is clear. Its
motto, "Let Love and Friendship Reign," is represented by
three distinct symbols joined in unity on the ring. As we
know, the hands signify faith in friendship, the crown loyalty,
and the heart signifies love. In Gaelic, the phrase *Gra Dilseacht,
agus Cairdeas*, pronounced phonetically as *Gra Deelshocked, ogis
Kordiss* means "Love, Loyalty, and Friendship." But the phrase
"Let Love and Friendship Reign" is the most commonly
accepted translation of the meaning of the Claddagh ring.

There have been countless interpretations over the years,
as author Cecily Joyce points out in her 1990 book, *The
Claddagh Ring Story*. Joyce notes that the hands signify faith,
trust or "plighted troth," and the heart not only includes love
but charity. The crown, along with loyalty, may symbolize
honor or "hope of future glory." Then, of course, there is the
poem, which makes it all easy to remember!

The hands are there for friendship,
The heart is there for love.
For loyalty throughout the year,
The crown is raised above.

More mythical in nature, one Celtic interpretation has *Dagda*, of *Dagda-Mor*, the powerful father of the gods, representing the right hand of the ring. It was Dagda who had the ability to stop the sun in its place, which he once did for nine straight months, according to legend. The mother of the Celts was known as Danu or Anu and represented the left hand, while Beathauile, not a person or a god but "life," is represented by the crown. The heart in this translation represents each and every person of mankind.

Yet another interpretation of the meaning of the ring corresponds to the Shamrock, which is one of the most ancient symbols of the Trinity among the Irish. The crown is interpreted as the Father, the left hand is the Son, and the right hand is the Holy Ghost, all of whom care for all of humanity, represented by the heart.

Despite the many variations of Claddagh ring designs, the presence of the hands, the heart, and the crown are what separate it from other "fede" or faith rings of ancient times. However, what is most uncommon about the Claddagh ring is the manner in which it can be worn. There is no telling how far these customs go back in time, and evidence would suggest that these options are more modern in practice, rather than ancient tradition. And yet, the very fact that people abide by them seriously when they get a Claddagh Ring is proof that the mystical nature of the ring is quite powerful and compelling.

Wearing the ring on the right hand with the crown turned inward to the wrist and the heart turned outward, indicates that your heart has not yet been taken. Wearing it on your right hand with the crown turned outward and the heart turned inward, indicates that you have made a commitment to someone. Wearing the Claddagh ring on your left hand with the crown turned outward and the heart turned inward, is an announcement that you have said "I do" and "I will" to your beloved.

While the significance of how the ring is worn may be more of a modern conception, fede rings, or "truth" rings, have been around since ancient Greek and Roman times, if not earlier. Fede rings usually featured two hands clasped together, and Roman examples have been dated back to 4 A.D. It was also believed that the Romans were the first to begin wearing these rings on the third or "ring" finger of the left hand. The Romans even coined the phrase *vena amoris*, which means "vein of love" and comes from the Egyptian theory that this "vein" led directly to the heart.

CHRISTIANITY IN IRELAND

To understand the Celtic influence on civilization and culture, it's important to understand the beginnings of

Christianity in Ireland. St. Patrick is the missionary who gets most of the credit for cultivating and spreading Christianity throughout Ireland, and while many historians believe that his missions may have been embellished and exaggerated, his contribution to Irish culture simply cannot be understated. Very little is known about Patrick. According to his "Confession," he was born in the early 400s A.D. in Roman Britain, probably in northern England, where his mother was a Gaul and his father an official with some family means. When Patrick was about sixteen, he was kidnapped, probably by Saxon or Pict raiders, and taken to Ireland where he was sold into slavery. It is believed that as a slave, he tended to sheep possibly in Mayo or Sligo and it was during this time in captivity that Patrick began praying, which continued for several years until he managed to escape.

Patrick is believed to have walked hundreds of miles across Ireland to the east coast, and then secured a spot on a ship to France (Gaul) where he began his training in earnest as a priest. According to his "Confession," he heard the call in his dreams, perhaps from God, to return to Ireland in 432, and he began roaming the Emerald Isle preaching the Gospel. Ireland at this time was holding many Celtic Pagan festivals, and Patrick set out to "Christianize" the masses—setting up churches and introducing religious order wherever he went—ultimately putting in place the Irish Church.

Along with Christianity, the production of books flourished in Ireland—replacing centuries of oral tradition, though some would argue that tradition has never wavered in the least! But the advent and proliferation of the written word in Ireland in the years following St. Patrick's return is considered one of the greatest contributions to civilization. The best known manuscript from this time is the Book of Kells— handwritten copies of the Bible and other books written in about 700 A.D. and illuminated by monks in Irish monasteries. Beautifully illuminated in painstaking detail, the Book of Kells is currently housed at Trinity College in Dublin.

At around the same time the monks were busy documenting and transcribing the word of God in these ornate manuscripts, the Gaels began arriving in Ireland *en masse,* having already spread across most of Europe. Like most conquering peoples, the Gaels brought with them their own cultural beliefs and established a new power structure in Ireland, but they also assimilated—intermarrying and establishing alliances within local and regional areas.

The fact that the Romans did not invade the Gaelic island had both advantages and disadvantages for the Irish culture. While it's true that the many Gaelic traditions have been preserved over centuries because they were never corrupted by Roman control, the country never witnessed many of the technological, agricultural, and military advances enjoyed by most European cultures after Roman conquest. Ireland became something of a safe haven for the cultivation of Christianity, and as the rest of Europe began to destruct under Roman rule, Ireland remained stable and even thrived as displaced scholars and intellects fled Europe. In short, Ireland did not experience Europe's dark ages, and later, when Christianity began to spread back to Europe, it was launched from the solid base of Ireland.

Joan Evans, in her book, *English Jewelry from the Fifth Century A.D. to 1800* (Methuen & Co. Ltd., 1921), explained this cultural impact in terms of art and scholarship. She wrote that Ireland became a European center of Christianity, and intellectual minds "flocked like bees" to Irish centers of study such as Durrow and Armagh. As these centers of study flourished, Celtic art acquired a new importance in Irish culture, Evans noted, as manuscripts, illuminated by "parchment and quill" eventually led to similar decorative patterns appearing in stone and metal arts of the time. Evans wrote:

> Regular compartments and open recessed panels were filled with exquisite interlaced work, and zoomorphic patterns of lacertine monsters and long-billed birds. The rich and varied ornament was controlled by a strong sense of line, proportion and relief; the ancient

traditions of pagan Celtic art remained too
strong for any barbarian roughness to survive
in the refinement of the Christian Celtic style.

The Irish artists demonstrated such skill that samples of
their work spread to Europe and before long, it was known
that the very best craftsmen of the ninth century, according
to Evans, "came from the Irish foundation of St. Gall." It was
very clear that some of the most common symbols in
Christian Celtic art—such as the trumpet, the animal, and the
spiral—symbols often seen in the ornate manuscripts of the
time, inspired goldsmiths as well. It was then, Evans wrote,
that artists created the Ardagh chalice, Bell-shrines, and the
popular penannular brooches "to represent the magnificence
and beauty of Christian Celtic metal work."

The penannular brooch is most notable. Evans believed
that these jeweled pieces, which were common in Ireland and
Scotland, were probably derived from a "pin with a wire bent
in a circle through the head." The penannular brooch is
unique in that the ring has a break in it (indicative of its
name) and this pin is longer than the diameter of the ring.
The wearer of the brooch would insert the pin into a
pinched piece of the clothing or fabric so that it would pass
between two points, then pull the pin through the break in
the ring and turn. This would keep the brooch in place and

secure it to the article of clothing. Evans also noted that the origins of many of these brooches have an element that could indeed be viewed as inspirational in design to the ring that would begin to appear centuries later.

> The penannular form is found at an early date in Ireland. Some VI century examples are of comparatively small size, and have the ends of the ring terminating in birds' heads. Later the finials became broader and flatter, and so shaped that only their outside edge conforms to a circle. These finials are often shewn issuing from the mouths of birds' heads, as in the silver-gilt ring of a penannular brooch of about 800 in the museum of the Royal Irish Academy. This shews the tendency to close the ring and make it only an ornamental appendage of the pin, which arose as soon as the decoration of the brooch became of more importance than its practical use . . .

These brooches from the sixth century have all the key ingredients of what would later become the Claddagh Ring, and it does not require much imagination to see where gold-smiths made the leap from bird's heads to two hands clasping a heart in these brooches. As Evans noted, development of the ring brooch that would appear in the later years of the 14th century was probably used as a love-token, with two clasped hands often holding a stone. A development of the ring brooch that arose in the later years of the 14th century, probably used as a love-token, has two tiny clasped hands, sometimes holding a stone, projecting from the ring.

In her book, Evans noted that marriage rings from the Middle Ages were different from ornamental rings only by the posy—the sentimental inscription on either the inner or outer portion of the ring. She also noted that "clasped hands are often found on betrothal rings, both gimmel and of the ordinary shape; one in the British Museum is inscribed on the shoulders with the posy 'God Help,' and is chased at the back with a heart and two quatrefoil flowers rising from it."

It is also thought that Celtics during the Middle Ages cut and braid human hair, wrap it around a finger or a wrist and wear it as a symbol of commitment. The "Gimmel" or "bond ring" was another ring of similar symbolism, as it consisted of two or sometimes three hoops that attached to the base of the ring. When worn around a finger, its appearance was that of a regular ring, but some historians have suggested that these rings may have been separated during the actual marriage ceremony as part of the vows or traditional union.

Vikings were known to have a fede ring that featured two hands clasped over the heart, practically covering it from view. Spain also had a similar design, and many suspect that Richard Joyce, while in captivity in Algiers, may have learned his craft making such rings. The Claddagh ring is certainly a member of the family of fede rings, which were quite popular during the Middle Ages and all over Europe, particularly in central and northern Italy during the Renaissance. These rings were also known as "betrothal rings" in the 16th century and there is little doubt that somehow, whether or not it was Richard Joyce himself, these rings influenced the design and making of Ireland's most symbolic ring.

George Frederick Kunz, in his 1917 book *Rings for the Finger* (J.B. Lippincott Company), observed that fede rings of this sort had not only worldwide appeal, but unique customs associated with them:

> Wedding rings figuring two clasped hands are still used by the peasants of Normandy, and in Galway also rings bearing two hands clasping a heart have been passed down from generation to generation, from the mother to the eldest daughter. This illustrates the general rule that long after a custom or a form of personal adornment has ceased to be in favor

with the high classes it continues to be popular with the peasantry.

In some parts of Ireland the belief in the special virtue of a gold wedding ring is so strong that when the bridegroom is too poor to buy one he will hire it for the occasion, and it is reported that a shopkeeper of Munster realized quite a little sum annually by renting rings for weddings, to be brought back to him after the ceremony. Strange to say, there is said to have been a superstitious fancy in Yorkshire, England, that to wed with a borrowed ring would bring good luck.

The Claddagh ring has come to represent more than just a betrothal ring. Grandmothers continue to give them to granddaughters as gifts whether or not a wedding is in the works. Grooms have been known to present them to their best men, and friends present them as friendship rings. Yet the rebirth and popularization of traditional Irish weddings around the world has led to a younger generation's appreciation for the ring that states, "Let Love and Friendship Reign."

TRADITIONAL IRISH WEDDINGS

A large and growing trend in contemporary marriage ceremonies in Europe and America is the traditional Irish wedding, and ironically, Richard Joyce, the legendary maker of the earliest known Claddagh rings and he who was captured by Algerian corsairs at the end of the 17th century, again takes center stage as we turn to this phenomenon. Clearly, Joyce's tale has been further embellished. Like all good legends, Richard's needed a little more romance to become even more compelling. In this tale, Richard was on the verge of being married to the girl of his dreams, when those swashbuckling Algerian corsairs descended on his boat, taking him prisoner and forcing him into slavery. Apparently, the corsairs knew not only how to spoil a nice wedding, but new and interesting methods of torturing the romantic soul. Richard Joyce was forced, as a slave in Algeria, to work as a goldsmith's apprentice, where he would spend the next fourteen years of his life making wedding bands and fede rings for more fortunate romantics than himself!

Finally, after King William III demanded that all British subjects be freed from captivity in Algiers, Joyce set sail for Galway, where he found that his maiden had never married and had passed the years dreaming and praying for her beloved's eventual return to Ireland. So exalted and humbled by the patience, devotion, and availability of his true love, Richard settled down to create the most beautiful ring he could possibly imaginable. The ring, as is known, depicts a bezel with two hands clasping a heart and a crown above.

This, the tale explains, is how the Claddagh ring was born.

As the traditional Irish wedding has become more popular, the Claddagh rings themselves have taken front and center stage. As implausible as many of these legends may seem, people on the verge of saying their vows become taken with the romance and the lore that make up a traditional Irish wedding. There are many different variations of traditional Irish weddings, too, ranging from ancient Gaelic customs to "capture weddings" and country weddings.

The famous Oscar Wilde had a mother named Jane Frances Wilde, a.k.a. J. Francesca Wilde, a.k.a. Speranza Francesca Wilde. But most people at the time referred to her as "Lady Wilde," and it was obvious to anyone who knew her that the apple (in this case, Oscar) did not fall far from the tree. Lady Wilde was an eccentric writer and poet in her time, in addition to being a highly charged Irish nationalist. However, in 1888, Ticknor & Company published her book, *Ancient Legends, Mystic Charms and Superstitions of Ireland.* In the book, Lady Wilde compiled a section entitled "Marriage Rites," and even she would be amused that many engaged couples and wedding planners look to this piece as something of a guidebook toward a traditional Irish wedding. It is worth reprinting at length.

MARRIAGE RITES

by Lady Wilde

From *Ancient Legends, Mystic Charms and Superstitions of Ireland,* Ticknor and Co., Boston, 1887

In old times in Ireland it was thought right and proper to seem to use force in carrying off the bride to her husband. She was placed on a swift horse before the bridegroom, while all her kindred started in pursuit with shouts and cries. Twelve maidens attended the bride, and each was placed on horseback behind the young men who rode after the bridal pair. On arriving at her future home, the bride was met on the threshold by her bridegroom's mother, who broke an oaten cake over her head a good augury of plenty in the future. In the mountains where horses cannot travel, the bridal party walk in procession; the young men carrying torches of dried bogwood to light the bride over the ravines, for in winter the mountain streams are rapid and dangerous to cross.

The Celtic ceremonial of marriage resembles the ancient Greek ritual in many points.

A traveler in Ireland some fifty years ago, before politics had quite killed romance and ancient tradition in the hearts of the people, thus describes a rustic marriage festival which he came on by chance one evening in the wilds of Kerry.

A large hawthorn tree that stood in the middle of a field near a stream was hung all over with bits of colored stuff, while lighted rush candles were placed here and there amongst the branches to symbolize, no doubt, the new life of brightness preparing for the bridal pair. Then came a procession of boys marching slowly with flutes and pipes made of hollow reeds, and one struck a tin can with a stick at intervals, with a strong rhythmical cadence. This represented the plectrum. Others rattled slates and bones between their fingers, and beat time, after the manner of the Crotolistori—a rude attempt at music, which appears amongst all nations of the earth, even the most savage. A boy followed, bearing a lighted torch of bogwood. Evidently he was Hymen, and the flame of love was his cognizance. After him came the betrothed pair hand-in-hand, a large square canopy of black stuff being held over their heads; the emblem, of course, of the mystery of love, shrouded and veiled from the prying light of day.

Behind the pair followed two attendants bearing high over the heads of the young couple a sieve filled with meal; a sign of the plenty that would be in their house, and an omen of good luck and the blessing of children.

A wild chorus of dancers and singers closed the procession; the chorus of the epithalamium, and grotesque figures, probably the traditional fauns and satyrs, nymphs and bacchanals, mingled together with mad laughter and shouts and waving of green branches.

The procession then moved on to a bonfire, evidently the ancient altar; and having gone round it three times, the black shroud was lifted from the bridal pair, and they kissed each other before all the people, who shouted and waved their branches in approval.

Then the preparations for the marriage supper began, on which, however, the traveler left them, having laid some money on the altar as an offering of good-will for the marriage's future. At the wedding supper, there was always plenty of eating and drinking, and dancing, and the feast was prolonged till near morning, when the wedding song was sung by the whole party of friends standing, while the bride and bridegroom remained seated at the head of the table. The chorus of one of these ancient songs may be thus literally translated from the Irish—

"It is not day nor yet day,
It is not day, nor yet morning:
It is not day, nor yet day,
For the moon is shining brightly"

Another marriage song was sung in Irish frequently, each verse ending with the lines—

"There is sweet enchanting music,
and the golden harps are ringing;
And twelve comely maidens deck
the bride-bed for the bride."

A beautiful new dress was presented to the bride by her husband at the marriage feast; at which also the father paid down her dowry before the assembled guests; and all the place round the house was lit by torches when night came on, and the song and the dance continued till daylight, with much speech-making and drinking of poteen. All fighting was steadily avoided at a wedding; for a quarrel would be considered a most unlucky omen. A wet day was also held to be very unlucky, as the bride would assuredly weep for sorrow throughout the year. But the bright warm sunshine was hailed joyfully, according to the old saying—

"Happy is the bride that the sun shines on;
But blessed is the corpse that the rain rains on."

Lady Wilde's romantic and mysterious description of an ancient Irish wedding appeals to a new generation of "traditionalists" who, even though they realize that some ceremonial aspects of the past are not practical today, still want to incorporate some simple and timeless elements into their wedding. Not every couple wants to bring a bonfire into the wedding, but aside from Claddagh rings being exchanged, there are some Irish customs and traditions that are making their way around the world as traditional Irish weddings become more popular.

Bagpipes, pennywhistles, fiddles, harps, and bodhrans (goatskin drums) all have a place in a traditional Irish wedding. It's the actual selection of Irish music that seems to overwhelm anyone who has tried to pick just a few special pieces. The "Irish Wedding Song," of course, often proves an irresistible choice. The success of the Irish productions of Bill Whelan's *Riverdance* has also inspired many couples to turn to traditional Irish dancers to "accessorize" their wedding.

For luck, the bride may carry a real horseshoe with the ends tipped up to keep the luck from running out. Porcelain models have since replaced real ones in most cases, or the shape of the horseshoe can be represented by fabric and wrapped on the bride's wrist. Aside from the bride wearing braided hair, the addition of flowers is another staple of traditional Irish weddings, as the flowers are often shaped into a wreath encircling the bride's head, a custom copied by many other cultures. And after the wedding, Bunratty Meade, a sweet honey wine from the Bunratty Castle in western Ireland, is considered the oldest drink in Ireland, and because of its quiet reputation as an aphrodisiac, has become something of a wedding banquet staple. In addition to the many different touches and customs, there are countless superstitions—similar in vein to the ones Claddagh fishermen adhered to when deciding whether to fish in Galway Bay on certain days. "Marry in May and rue the day" is one phrase linked to Irish luck and misfortune, yet ironically, May is the most popular month for weddings in Ireland! Another saying, "Marry in April if you can, joy for maiden and for man," lingers there to help couples guide some of their important wedding decisions!

There are other traditions, such as the "janting char" in which the groom is carried in a chair as he is presented to the guests at the reception, which is also a feature of Jewish weddings. And for the honeymoon, *mi na meala* in Irish, meaning the month of honey, it was the custom for newlyweds to seclude themselves from family and friends, drinking wine or mead and hoping to avoid being separated by the families. This was a common occurrence in ancient Irish times, as young couples would elope as part of the tradition leading up to the marriage ceremony. Even the villagers of the Claddagh adhered to a version of this *mi na meala*.

Other Irish superstitions include:

It's bad luck to marry on a Saturday.

Seeing three magpies or hearing a cuckoo on the morning of a wedding is good luck.

Avoid breaking a glass on the wedding day.

Avoid funeral processions at any time on the wedding day.

When the bride leaves the church with the groom, an old

shoe should be tossed over her head for good luck. (This should be done by someone other than bride or groom.)

The bride's new mother-in-law should break a piece of wedding cake (preferably an Irish whiskey cake) on the bride's head as she enters the house after the wedding, making the two friends for life.

Of all the customs, superstitions, traditions, and music inherent in the many versions of a traditional Irish wedding, there seems to be one thing that remains consistent and present in each wedding—the exchange of the Claddagh rings. A trip to Thomas Dillon's in Galway, which was established in 1750 and is the city's original maker of the Claddagh ring, is often a mandatory stop for engaged couples to visit when shopping for a traditional Claddagh ring. Dillon's is also home to the Claddagh Museum, which holds the oldest Claddagh rings in existence and is a remarkable source for researching the traditional Irish wedding—especially if you find variation in Claddagh rings inspiring. A walk through the museum is a reminder of what the ring symbolizes and the strength of that symbol, as Claddagh rings centuries old are presented. The tools used to make these ancient rings are also on display, and one can't help but imagine Richard Joyce, back in Ireland after his ordeal at the hands of Algerian corsairs, using tools such as these to create the ring his wife would wear as an everlasting symbol of love, loyalty, and friendship.

Jonathan Margetts is the owner of Thomas Dillon's, and the shop has been in the Margetts family since his grandfather Patrick purchased it from William Dillon in 1920. Jonathan himself has been with Dillon's for over 30 years, going into the jewelry business "straight out of school, when I was sixteen." Margetts made the headlines of Irish newspapers a few years ago when nearly a dozen Claddagh rings had been lost, and he arrived at the Ballinasloe Landfill, donning rubber boots and gloves, and began sifting through the rubbish in search of the rings, which had been freshly engraved for family members and friends. Miraculously, the rings were found in a pile that was just about to be compacted, and the story had a very happy ending for all involved.

The Claddagh Museum, sometimes referred to as "the smallest museum in Europe," has been open for over ten years now. Aside from the early Claddagh rings on display, one of the most popular exhibits is the "world's smallest Claddagh ring," which can be viewed through a magnifying glass. "I made it myself," Margetts said. "We weren't very busy one day, and out of boredom, I just decided to see how small I could make one."

The people who come to the museum are "fascinated with the village," Margetts said. Some have a romantic vision of the Claddagh as a place where "everyone is sitting fireside, rosy-eyed," and the museum offers not only the early Claddagh rings, but vintage photographs, articles, and artifacts from as far back as the Stone Age, showing the life in that mysterious village on the banks of Galway Bay.

Of course, the rings are made differently from the way they were when Richard Joyce was crafting Claddagh rings by hand. No longer are the rings made with "cuttle-shell" casting. Today's rings are one-piece cast and much stronger. Margetts also notes that most of the rings he's making these days are 14 carat. "Years ago," he said, "gold was low and people wanted lighter rings. But now, they want the rings to be heavy and last a lifetime."

Margetts is also seeing people from all walks of life come into his shop for Claddagh rings. "We have much more interest from college students now," he said, echoing a theme of the Claddagh ring, that new generations will continue to be intrigued and captivated by a timeless symbol of love, loyalty, and friendship. Dillon's has also sold rings to numerous dignitaries and celebrities over the years, including Walt Disney, John Wayne, Bing Crosby, and President John F. Kennedy. The shop and the museum on 1 Quay Street in Galway City is an essential stop for anyone looking to step into the past.

CHAPTER V

She wore it a lifetime and gave it to me.

The Claddagh Ring Endures

WHEN IN GALWAY, take a walk down Quay Street in front of the Spanish Arch. Then cross the River Corrib and you'll be on Claddagh Quay, heading toward Nimmo's Pier. Sadly, there is not much left from the days when the King of the Claddagh determined on which days the Claddagh men would fish, but the pier itself remains. Standing there and looking out toward Galway Bay, toward Mutton Island where the fisherman of the Claddagh could always count on a bountiful catch, you'll get a sense of that same timeless view. Little has changed, when you look out over the bay. The geese that flocked in great numbers to the area along the River Corrib—well, their descendants are still here, though in lesser numbers. You can almost see the barefoot Claddagh women in their plain red gowns with their children, walking along the strand, collecting worms for their husbands to use as bait. Let the imagination run riot as you take a walk at sunset. It's allowable to get sentimental and nostalgic for a past you don't know or never had, and to find yourself humming the doleful tune of Galway Bay, and maybe mouthing the words:

> And it may be some day I'll go back to Ireland,
> If it's only at the closing of the day,
> Just to see again the moon rise over Claddagh,
> And watch the sun go down on Galway Bay.

The people of the Claddagh are gone now, and the area has been newly developed, with new houses standing where the village of Claddagh stood for centuries. Ireland has undergone a tremendous change in recent years—an economic boom transforming the country into the "Celtic Tiger." No longer are the young Irish emigrating in waves. In fact, immigration to Ireland has been the recent trend, as more and more dreamers from abroad flow into the country in hope of finding work. Galway is a city of youth. Walk a few blocks down its busiest streets and you might not encounter a single person above the age of forty. With 7,000 or so college students living in the city, and countless others who come either for career opportunities, or the bustling pub scene and lively restaurants, the city of Galway may well represent the energy and ideals of a new generation of Irish. They are young men and women who perhaps do not know very much about a place just a stone's throw from where they work and shop and meet for drinks—a place called the Claddagh—indeed, little curiosity is evinced in any local history. Getting on, as they say in Ireland, is the thing.

And while they may not be familiar with Margaret of the Bridges or Richard Joyce or Algerian corsairs or the King of the Claddagh, they are almost all familiar with the meaning and the symbolism of the Claddagh ring. Go into any Irish pub in Galway on a busy night and you'll need more than two hands to count the Claddagh rings. This is not a culture that sneers at a tradition some might view as unsophisticated or quaint. They know what the Claddagh ring stands for and they embrace it wholly—male and female. Women wear it as a gift from a boyfriend, a mother, a grandmother, and even a close girlfriend. Men receive Claddagh rings from grooms after serving as best men at weddings, or from girlfriends or even fathers. The symbol of love and friendship is so strong— the Claddagh design has even become a popular tattoo for those who seek a permanent commitment.

Seeing all these young, ebullient, and friendly Irish souls with Claddagh rings made it difficult not to think of those smiling faces on the missing persons fliers posted all over the streets of New York in the days and weeks following September 11, 2001. Maybe it just seemed that way, but the people wearing Claddagh rings around the world appear to carry so much hope with them. With the ring around their finger, they are proclaiming that they are loved, and that they love in return. They believe in loyalty and friendship with all their heart, and they are not afraid or ashamed of sharing that with anyone.

Sometime after those attacks on the twin towers, a story made its way around the city about a New York police officer who perished at Ground Zero. The officer was last seen pulling victims from the World Trade Center, and then going back into the buildings to save more people. When things were looking pretty dismal, this cop could have said, "That's enough, I have a two-year-old daughter at home I'd like to see again." But this was a New York City cop—selfless, dedicated, and heroic to the very end. This cop's name was Moira Smith, and she was the only female NYPD officer to lose her life in the attacks.

Instead of celebrating her 39th birthday with her husband James and her young daughter, Patricia Mary, family and friends gathered together at St. Patrick's Cathedral in Manhattan on Valentine's Day of 2002 to memorialize this courageous fallen hero. Just two months before, little Patricia Mary had accompanied her father on the stage at Carnegie Hall to accept the Medal of Honor—the highest award that can be bestowed upon a member of the service—where the young girl heartbreakingly accepted the medal for the mother she would never see again.

The city of New York, however, was not done honoring this heroic member of New York's Finest. In February 2002, a new high-speed ferry that runs up and down the East River was christened the *Moira Smith* and hundreds of family and friends gathered at a pier just blocks from Ground Zero for the ceremony. Painted on the bow of the boat alongside the name was the Claddagh ring symbol, added at the request of the family. This was a symbol Moira Smith shared with her husband James, as the two exchanged Claddagh rings as wedding bands at their marriage in 1998.

When James Smith rose to honor his wife at the boat's christening, his words were those that have been spoken for generations, and yet it would be difficult to find a more heartbreaking and poignant moment in the history of the Claddagh ring.

"This design embodies Moira's spirit," James Smith said. "There's a traditional saying that goes with the giving of a Claddagh: With these hands I give you my heart, and I crown it with my love."

So it may be said that the Claddagh ring embodies love and hope and friendship and heartbreak, making it a symbol not just of those qualities and emotions, but also of life itself. Because of the surging popularity of the ring, it seems unlikely that the Claddagh ring will ever experience another dormant period, the way it did after Richard Joyce retired from the goldsmith business almost three hundred years ago. Repeat after me: "Let Love and Friendship Reign."

Slainte.

BIBLIOGRAPHY

Anbinder, Tyler. *Five Points: The 19th-century New York City Neighborhood That Invented Tap Dance, Stole Elections, and Became the World's Most Notorious Slum*, New York, 2001

Banim, Mary. *Here and There Through Ireland*, Dublin, 1892

Cronin, Mike. *A History of Ireland*, Houndmills, Basingstoke, Hampshire; New York, 2001

Delamer, Ida. "The Claddagh Ring," in *Irish Arts Review Yearbook*, XII, 1996

De Latocnaye. *A Frenchman's Walk Through Ireland 1796-7*, Cork, 1798

Dillon, William. "The 'Claddagh' Ring," in *Journal of Galway Archaeological & Historical Society Journal*, IV, 1905–6

Dwyer, Jim. "Sonofagun, if It Isn't Dominion," in *The New York Times*, November 11, 2001

Evans, Joan. *English Jewelry from the Fifth Century A.D. to 1800*, London, 1921

Hall, A.M. & S.C. Ireland, *Its Scenery and Character*, London, 1842

—*Hand-book to Galway, Connamara and the Irish Highlands*, London, 1854

Hardiman, James. *History of the Town and County of Galway*, Galway, 1820

Joyce, Cecily. *The Claddagh Ring Story*, Galway, 1990

Kunz, George Frederick. *Rings for the Finger*, Philadelphia, 1917

Lewis, Samuel. *A Topographical Dictionary of Ireland*, Dublin, 1837

Lovett, Richard. *Irish Pictures*, 1888

Macken, Walter. *Rain on the Wind*, Dingle, Co. Kerry, 1950

McMahon, Sean. *The Story of the Claddagh Ring*, Dublin, 1999

O'Dowd, Paedar. *Down by the Claddagh*, Galway, 1993

O'Dowd, Paedar. *Vanishing Galway*, Galway, 1987

Quinn, Reverend George. "The Claddagh Ring," *The Mantel*. Vol XII No. 1 Spring 1970

Rodenberg, Julius, *The Island of the Saints; a Pilgramage through Ireland*, London, 1861

Villiers–Tuthill, Kathleen. *Beyond the Twelve Bens*, Dublin, 1986

Wilde, Lady. *Ancient Legends, Mystic Charms, and Superstitions of Ireland*, Boston, 1887

Young, Arthur. *A Tour in Ireland (1776-1778)*, London, 1780